Published by

Luckypuddle Publishing 2008
Copyright © Sally Bee 2008

Photography By Dogan Halil
Photographs copyright © Dogan Halil 2008
Front Cover By Mike Horseman © Mike Horseman 2008

Sally Bee h͟   erted her right under the copyright, designs and patents act 1988 to be
identified as   author of this work. Apart from where, kind permission has been given by
ned contributors to use their words, names and/or recipes.

www.sally-bee.com

www.luckypuddlepublishing.com

ISBN 978-0-9559007-0-9

End   from the sale of this book will go to the British Heart Foundation.
/ Bee has pledged to raise £1 Million pounds over 5 years
for the British Heart Foundation.

www.bhf.org.uk

Printed by
Adlard Print & Reprographics Limited
The Old School, The Green, Ruddington, Nottingham NG11 6HH

XB00 000000 0946

WOLVERHAMPTON
LIBRARIES

Sally Bee is a cook with a difference and a special story to tell. After suffering from a rare heart condition that caused her to have 3 heart attacks at the age of 36, healthy food became not just a passion but a necessity for her future. Having amazed her doctors with her survival and subsequent recovery, Sally loves nothing more than cooking up a storm for her friends, family and clients that is beyond healthy and nutritious. Sally's mission is to prove again and again that food can offer a true nutritional benefit and at the same time be deliciously tempting, heavenly and scrumptious! Mood Food - herbs by the handful, adventurous and exotic, inventive flavours to tempt any palate. Sally Bee's dishes are easy to prepare and are a treat for the mind, body and soul.

"I believe that appearances can be deceptive and although I look fit and well now, busy about town with my 3 young children, at one point I was in a pretty bad way and my husband was sent to me to say goodbye. None of the medics thought I could possibly survive the damage my heart had sustained - but then hey, I always did believe in miracles. And now almost 4 years on, I still amaze the medics with the great progress that I am making. Obviously because of my health issues I need to eat really well. And actually, I now believe in what I call 'active eating'. This is simple, but for me, incredibly effective. Not only do I avoid the things that I know are bad for me like fat, sugar and salt, I also actively include the ingredients that I know have a good health benefit for me and give me a boost.

All my recipes are easy to follow and as I'm not a chef, please believe me when I say that if I can make these healthy dishes, anyone can make them!

Many of us know the principles of healthy eating, but actually producing a healthy meal at the end of a busy day, that the whole family can enjoy, can be a bit of a daunting task. I hope that my recipes give you a little inspiration and show you how easy it is to take control of your future health and the health of your family."

WOLVERHAMPTON PUBLIC LIBRARIES	
XB000000000946	
Bertrams	08/06/2009
641.5BEE	£9.99
SV 13/6	533411

My Story

My story begins on a lovely sunny, happy day, spent at a childs birthday party. Talking to my friends, laughing and watching the children play. One moment everything was just as it should be, but within one breath my whole life was turned upside down never to be the same again.

I was sitting around a table, chatting to friends when I suddenly began to feel very poorly. I handed my 9 month old baby girl to a friend, and ran to the toilet. I had feeling of impending doom as if a big black cloud was looming over me making every breath more meaningful. I understood immediately that something serious was happening to me and it was beyond my control. I collapsed on the floor and I felt like my chest was being crushed and I was struggling to breathe. I felt sick and hot and sweaty. The pain I was enduring was so much worse than giving birth to any of my three babies. Above all, I had a feeling somewhere deep inside of me that this was very serious. Chaos quickly ensued all around. An ambulance was called and while we waited, my friends were trying to help me, bringing me ice, water and a bag to breathe into. All I did was stare at my husband's eyes because I needed him to be with me and to understand what I was saying to him. I managed to give him some brief instructions on what to do with the children but I guess I was telling him something much more than that too.

The ambulance arrived, and the crew checked me over. They managed to calm me down a little and took an ECG. (A measurement of the heart beat.) They said there was a slight abnormality, but because of my young age, 36, and the fact that there was no family history of heart problems and I led a very healthy lifestyle, they were happy to rule out any serious heart problems there and then. However, it was felt that I should go to the Accident and Emergency Department to get properly checked out.

After a few hours spent at A&E, I was eventually let home with some indigestion medicine.

I spent the next couple of days recovering at home, feeling traumatised by the whole event. I couldn't put my finger on it, but I felt something had changed inside me. A couple of days later, after clearing up the tea remains, the pain hit me again. Feeling like a heard of elephants stamping on my chest! My breath was tight and so incredibly painful. If at that moment someone had said that by cutting off my right arm, the pain would go away, I would have passed them the knife!

Events at the hospital this time started to unravel like a really bad soap opera.

It started with pure panic. I was not being taken seriously and I was left alone in my cubicle suffering in agony. I couldn't call anyone to come and help me because the pain literally took my breath away. I thought I might die alone in a cubicle and not be found for hours. Eventually one student nurse looked at my ECG and her jaw dropped

Suddenly, I was no longer alone. The room was buzzing with people all around me. At one point I had three cardiologists looking at my heart trace chart saying that it was telling them I was having a heart attack but they didn't believe it because of my age, lifestyle etc.

I was told by a cardiologist the next morning that my blood tests showed that I had in fact suffered a very serious heart attack. At this time, I felt numb with disbelief but relieved that I had survived. Apparently I got really cross with the doctor for talking such rubbish! I just wanted to go home.

Unfortunately that was not going to happen for quite a while. Throughout the day I started to suffer more chest pains. I could feel myself sinking lower and lower and I kept being moved from one bed to another, closer and closer to the Cardiac Care Unit. I needed to be monitored constantly and apparently my heart rhythm was doing some quite amazing acrobatics. A nurse was sent to take a scan of my heart. I suppose it is down to my natural optimism that I still expected her to say, 'oh everything's fine.... probably eaten something dodgy!' But her expression was grave. She has since told me that she was so shocked to see the most damage she has ever seen on anyone so young.

I continued to deteriorate and was eventually wheeled into the coronary care high dependency unit. This was a room that has a very different feel about it. All white, very tall ceilings, voices echo. The beds have very wide spaces between them to accommodate the 'teams' of doctors and nurses that come to your rescue. My 'team' came to my rescue at about 5pm. I had sunk so low, the pain in my chest was breaking through the drugs they had given me and I could no longer talk. The only thought in my head was to keep breathing. Breathe in and breathe out, breathe in, breathe out. I figured if I could just keep breathing I wouldn't die. The doctors and nurses were quickly putting needles and lines into both of my arms and hands. The team were all moving very quickly around me using hushed voices. I managed to whisper to one of the nurses as she crouched at my bedside and held my hand. She held a look of great pity. She said they were calling my husband to come back. He'd gone home to be with the children for teatime. I asked if I was going to die now, and she swallowed hard before saying 'not now' but gave her colleague a look. She was a lovely gentle nurse but no good at telling lies.

The team managed to stabilise me enough to move me to another hospital where, they said, I would get fixed up. They expected that I must have a blockage somewhere in my heart that was causing the heart attack and had arranged for me to have an angiogram.

This is where they put a tube up through a vein in your groin, into the heart. Dye is pumped into the heart and an x-ray shows the blood and oxygen flow or subsequent blockage. If there is a blockage it can often be cleared by fitting a stent or performing a bypass.

I think at this point I was in and out of consciousness. I was aware that I was just hanging on and wasn't at all sure how long I could hang on for. We arrived at the new hospital and the surgeon, who had been dragged out of bed, told me all the risks associated with an angiogram and the mortality rate. Even in my perilous state I could do the maths and thought there were other things I would rather be doing.

The cath lab was very cold and I had to lie on an even colder table to have the angiogram done. By this point I was relatively relaxed. Partly due to the drugs I had been given but also partly down to what was happening to my body. I think I was starting to shut down. I felt myself let go a couple of times and it frightened me…. but it was not unpleasant. It would have been very easy to just drift off. I knew my situation was very bad and the thing that surprises me was how calm I was by now. The Surgeon started his procedure putting an incision in my groin. I felt the blood trickle over my leg. He then fed the line up into my heart to pump the dye in and x-ray the results. I've said that I felt very close to the edge. I was still quietly determined to just keep breathing, but I almost gave up when I heard the surgeon start to swear under his breath. I looked at his face and saw an expression of shock and disbelief and then panic and then nothing. When the surgeon started to swear, I think I began to understand just how dire my situation was. Having said this, I still wasn't prepared for what happened next. Everyone went away. Upped and left. Gone. Alone. I was left completely and utterly alone in this dreadful room on this cold table. The Surgeon took off his gloves, leaving with his shoulders drooped, the nurses and assistants all left the room quietly as if they were embarrassed and I was all alone. I actually thought for a moment that I was dead and this was what it was like. I stopped forcing my breath and let my natural breath take over. It was so shallow and light but it was all I could hear in the room. I couldn't fill my lungs. Was I still alive? I could drift off really easily and when I did the pain in my chest went away. I did it a couple of times to see what it was like. It was fine. Just fine. I would then pull myself back and the hurting returned, but it had turned into a 'good pain' because it proved that I was still alive. I really needed that confirmation. And I really needed to feel the pain.

After what seemed like a couple of hours, but probably only a couple of minutes, Dogan, my husband, walked into the room. He was sobbing. He told me that he loved me. The doctors had told him that I had suffered another massive heart attack and that my heart had sustained a shocking amount of damage that could not be repaired. They told him that I was going to die. So as he walked in the operating room, he was coming to say goodbye.

I would love to be able to write that I told him how much I loved him and we held each other tight. That didn't happen. Since I had just discovered, that I was still alive, and I'd allowed myself to think for a second about my little ones at home, I was filled with an all consuming need and desire and passion not to let myself die. I can't put into words how strong this feeling was. It was this surge of emotion that literally saved my life. It must have been all about the people that I love. It was instinctive and I decided there and then that I would never, ever give up breathing.

I had so much to live for. X

EATING FOR HEALTH

Well, as you have probably gathered, having survived the un-survivable, my future health became so very important to me. I was told how lucky I was to still be here, and because my condition is so rare, and is usually only diagnosed in post-mortem, nobody could give me a good prognosis for long term survival. Therefore it was blindingly obvious to me that I was the only person who could control how long I was to be around! And let me tell you ....I'm not done yet!

What had actually happened to my heart was something so rare, that none of the Cardiologists that I have seen subsequently have ever actually dealt with it before. My main left artery, the one inside the heart that feeds the heart muscle the blood and oxygen had literally unraveled and fallen apart. The condition is called 'Spontaneous Coronary Artery Dissection'. My artery just simply fell apart which meant that the blood coming into the heart, instead of being pumped straight out to feed my body was actually just leaking away. My heart was literally bleeding and being starved of the blood and oxygen that it needed to function and my body and other vital organs were also being starved. I had just enough output, or blood trickling through to keep me alive. Just.

So, its pretty important that not only do I keep fit through exercise, but that I eat well too. In fact throughout my recovery, I have really learnt to listen to my body and it tells me that when I eat fresh, healthy ingredients I feel well, I have more energy and I don't get quite as many side effects from my heart condition. I also realised pretty quickly that when I eat processed food or junk food I feel lethargic, my heart rate rises, often with uncomfortable palpitations and I generally lose my feeling of wellbeing. At the same time as having to take care of my own body, I have three young children and a husband to feed. Not wanting to make different meals for everyone I had to learn how to come up with dishes that would give me the best health benefit possible and tempt the kids and keep everyone smiling!

Meal times in our home have always been very lively, family affairs, with all of us sitting down at the table together. Lots of chatter and clatter! Taking this into consideration, if I even attempted to sit my lot down in front of a jacket potato and salad, they'd all jump up and leave home faster than you could say "but cottage cheese is good for you!"

Therefore, my recipes are not only healthy and simple to make, they are also meals that will satisfy the tastebuds of grown-ups and kids alike. There are plenty of old family favourites, made in a healthy way, and a few new tastes to try too.

Food needs to satisfy our mind, body and soul. We all need to feel that we've treated ourselves to something delicious that we deserved. We want to feel full up at the end of a meal - not still hungry. This is why diets don't work. If you feel you are depriving yourself of something day in, day out, you are eventually going to crack and go and fill up on all the junk that is so bad for you. If you think about it, all our happiest memories are in some way related to food; A birthday meal, Christmas lunch, lovers sharing dinner together. Life is too short to live 'on a diet' but by eating delicious, tasty food everyday that offers us a great health benefit, not only are we satisfying our souls we are treating ourselves to more energy, youthful looks and hopefully, a longer, healthier life.

Enjoy. X

REFLECTIVE

Good old fashioned family favourites with a healthy twist.

Don't always assume that a 'healthy' meal has to be based on a jacket potato or salad . . . life is short and our appetites can be big. Sometimes we need comfort food to fill us up. These dishes are based on some that you'll remember from your childhood - but you may have forgotten how easy they are to make from scratch with fresh, healthy, delicious ingredients.

Chicken Casserole

Potatoes a la Patrick

Healthy Lasagne

Hearty Shepherds Pie

Sardines on Toast

Bangers and Mash

Healthy Egg and Chips!!

*This book is dedicated to my 3 little food-tasters
– who are incredibly critical !!!
Tarik, Kazim and Lela.
xxx*

CHICKEN CASSEROLE

This dish is easy-peasy but so delicious my whole family demand it at least once a week. My boys like to make it into a pie, by simply baking some puff pastry 'lids' separately in the oven and serving them on top of the casserole. It's simple enough to have mid week without too much fuss, with a good helping of brown or basmati rice and lots of green veg. *(I love asparagus with it!).*

Serves 4

2 tbsp extra virgin olive oil	2 cloves garlic, crushed
6 rashers very lean bacon, cubed	2 tbsp plain flour
4-6 chicken breast portions without skin	Sprinkle of dried mixed herbs
2 organic courgettes – sliced	10 fl oz chicken or vegetable stock
1 red pepper – sliced	10 fl oz white wine
8oz shallots, peeled and halved if large	Black pepper

- Gently heat the olive oil in a large flameproof casserole dish. Add the bacon and fry until golden. Drain on absorbent kitchen paper.

- Mix the plain flour with some black pepper and the dried mixed herbs in a large bowl, and dust the chicken breasts.

- Brown the chicken as you did the bacon, then add the shallots and garlic, sauté for 2-3 mins.

- Now add all remaining ingredients, vegetables, cooked bacon, stock and wine. If you like your casserole sauce to be a little thicker, mix the remaining flour with a little of the stock and mix in well.

- Cover and cook in the oven at 170ºC (325ºF) gas mark 3 for about 1 1/2 hours or until tender.

Quick tip: If towards the end of cooking you feel the sauce has reduced too much, just add a little more stock!

Roast Potatoes A La Patrick

One of my neighbours, Patrick, taught me how to do these scrumptious yet very easy roast potatoes before I could even boil an egg. We had them round at his house once and they were amazing. This recipe does use salt which I usually avoid but as long as you've cut down on all processed food with added salt, a little bit with your fresh food every now and then will do you no harm

Fresh organic potatoes, peeled, halved and quartered.

Extra Virgin Olive Oil

2/3 sprigs fresh rosemary

Celery Salt

Onion Salt

Garlic Powder

- Prepare how ever many potatoes you would normally for the amount of mouths you are about to feed.

- No need to par-boil the potatoes. Place in a roasting tray and drizzle with the olive oil so that the potatoes are glistening all over but not drenched! Next, sprinkle with the celery salt, onion salt and garlic powder. Make sure that all potatoes have a light dusting of these flavours. Add the sprigs of fresh rosemary and put into the oven, pre-heated to 200°c, turning occasionally for about an hour.

- When finished the potatoes should be nicely browned.

This recipe isn't just limited to potatoes, you can roast carrots and parsnips in the same way, or all jumbled in together – gorgeous!

*Big Tip: Use a 'magic carpet' available from Lakeland. This is a non-stick sheet that you cut to fit your roasting tin and stops anything and everything from sticking. It means you can use less olive oil, as you don't need any to lubricate the tin, only to glisten on the vegetables.

HEALTHIEST-EVER LASAGNE

Serves 4

- Heat the oil in a large saucepan over a low heat. Add the onion and fry gently for 5 minutes. Add the carrots, celery and garlic and cook for a further 5 minutes until the onion is soft and just beginning to colour.

- Turn up the heat a little, then add the beef or turkey and cook, stirring and breaking up the meat with a wooden spoon until browned and crumbly. Add the mushrooms and cook for 1 more minute. (drain off any fat from the meat)

- Stir in the stock, wine or extra stock, tomatoes, tomato purée and dried herbs. Bring to the boil, then cover and gently simmer over a low heat for 45 minutes, stirring occasionally. Stir in the parsley and season to taste. Preheat the oven to 200°C.

- To make the sauce, mix the cornflour to a smooth paste with a little of the milk. Heat the remaining milk to boiling point, then pour some of it onto the cornflour mixture, stirring. Return this to the milk in the saucepan. Bring to the boil, stirring until the sauce thickens, then simmer for 2 minutes. Stir in the nutmeg and season to taste.

Lowri Turner

Lowri is a well-known journalist, TV presenter and author, Lowri is a regular guest on The Wright Stuff on Channel 5 and she writes for The Mail on Sunday and First Magazine.

I asked Lowri what her favourite ingredients and dish are.

"I am one of 5 children and supper in our house was complicated as we all ate different things. One brother was vegetarian, another hated vegetables, my sister and I ate hardly anything at all. However, the one meal my mother made that we all ate was lasagne - even my veggie brother! Lasagne now sums up comfort food for me."

Heart Felt Thanks To Lowri Turner

Spoon half the meat sauce over the base of a 3 litre ovenproof dish or roasting tin. Cover with a layer of lasagne, then spoon over the remaining meat sauce and cover with another layer of pasta.

Pour over the white sauce to cover the lasagne completely. Scatter over the grated cheese.

Place the dish on a baking sheet and bake for 40-45 minutes until the lasagne is bubbling and the top is lightly browned. Remove from the oven and leave to settle for 10 minutes before serving.

Serve with a lovely big salad

2 tbsp extra virgin olive oil	400g can chopped tomatoes
1 large onion, finely chopped	4 tbsp tomato purée
4 organic carrots, scrubbed but skin on and finely chopped	1 tbsp dried oregano or mixed herbs
	Handful of chopped fresh parsley
2 organic celery sticks, finely chopped	10 sheets dried no-pre-cook lasagne
2 garlic cloves, crushed	40g mature cheddar cheese, grated
350g lean minced steak or turkey mince	*Sauce:*
150g button mushrooms, chopped	3 tbsp cornflour
300ml beef stock or chicken stock	600ml semi-skimmed milk
150ml red wine or extra beef stock	Pinch of freshly grated nutmeg

HEARTY SHEPHERDS PIE

I decided that I must include this dish as a 'reflective' recipe because it is an old tradition in many households. My mum used to make it for us on a cold day. I love my mum more than the world but I have to tell you that cooking isn't her strong point. At least she always knows who her true friends are – those that came back for her company, despite the food. Having said that, her shepherds pie was pretty good . . . However, as a child I was never too excited about eating it until I tucked in. It's one of those dishes that you might class as boring but if you get it right and are starving hungry, there is actually nothing better! (Especially with a dollop of tomato ketchup on top!) There are many different ingredients that could be added to a Shepherds Pie and I was lucky enough to be allowed into the 'inner circle' and discover just what Jeffrey Archers secret ingredient is. I have to admit that it works a treat. I've adapted his personal recipe slightly, cutting out all extra oil that is not necessary and of course there is no salt. I've also included a couple of extra herbs and plenty of garlic for added flavour.

Great Tip : Super Mashed Potato Many of our old traditional dishes involve mashed potato like bangers and mash, shepherds pie and fish pie. Creamy mashed potato is warm and comforting and my children love it just on it's own with lots of gorgeous onion gravy. You can see from the Shepherds pie recipe that I don't add any fat or salt to the mash. This really isn't necessary if you use plenty of sweet potatoes. Sweet potatoes are much softer and they hold their moisture better than white potatoes. All you need to do is add a splash of milk and by using an electric whisk you will get lovely fluffy light mashed potato with hardly any fat content.
You can add anything to flavour the mash; wholegrain mustard, rosemary, oregano, thyme, spring onions, caramelised onions or fennel and cumin seeds give a really exotic taste. Give it a go!

Jeffrey Archer

Jeffrey wrote and told me that his all time favourite dish is Shepherds Pie. I was quite surprised by this and suppose I expected him to go for something a little more sophisticated. He says it reminds him of Christmas as it is always served at his annual Christmas parties.

Umm, original idea.

Heart Felt Thanks To Jeffrey Archer

Serves 4-5

600g (1.5 lbs) potatoes
(peeled and diced)

600g (1.5 lbs) sweet potato
(peeled and diced)

black pepper (to taste)

3 tablespoons semi-skimmed milk

400g (16oz) Extra lean minced lamb or
beef or turkey.

1 medium onion (peeled and chopped)

1 stick of celery, chopped

2 cloves garlic, crushed or chopped

1 desert spoon plain flour

440g (17oz) can chopped tomatoes

$1/2$ pint vegetable stock

1 slug of Worcester sauce

2 bay leaves

Jeffrey Archers secret ingredient :
1 tsp mango chutney!

Handful fresh rosemary, chopped

Handful fresh Oregano, chopped

Or good sprinkling of dried herbs if fresh
not available.

Boil potatoes and sweet potatoes for 15-20 minutes, or until tender.
Drain and mash with the milk using an electric whisk until smooth. Season with pepper.

Dry fry the minced lamb, beef or chicken until browned.
Drain off any excess fat, add the onion, celery and garlic and fry for a further 3-4 minutes, stirring occasionally.

Sprinkle over the flour and stir until the mince and onion mixture is evenly coated.

Add the tin of tomatoes, the herbs and half pint of vegetable stock. Bring to the boil, stirring until thickened. Reduce the heat, cover and simmer for 20 minutes, stirring occasionally.

Place mince in a heatproof dish. Spoon the mashed potato mixture over the top. Texture the topping with a fork.

Either grill until lightly browned, or pop into a pre-warmed oven (200C/400F/Gas mark 6) for 20 minutes.

SARDINES ON TOAST

Sardines are packed with goodness and make a really quick and easy snack. We used to have them for sunday tea sometimes, either that or toasted crumpets with butter. However, no matter how hard I try, I cannot come up with a suitably healthy version of buttered crumpets , so sardines on toast, for Sunday tea, it is.

Serves 4

120g can sardines in tomato sauce

1 celery stick, finely chopped

1/2 red pepper, finely chopped

1 Spring onion, thinly sliced

1 tbsp sun-dried tomato paste

2 tbsp lime juice

4 thick slices wholemeal or multigrain bread

Sprig watercress or olives to garnish

- Lightly break up the sardines in a bowl with a fork. Add the chopped celery, red pepper, onion, tomato paste and lime juice to the sardines. Season lightly with celery salt and freshly ground black pepper.

- Toast the bread slices on both sides until golden. Spoon the sardine mixture on top. Serve immediately.

BANGERS AND MASH

Everyone's a winner! Kids are happy, grandparents are happy, so you are happy. Who doesn't love Bangers and mash?

A healthy dish? Absolutely! Done in the right way this can be eaten with no guilt attached.

Sausages* - The Rules:

Only buy sausages from your local reputable butcher. Not supermarket, cheap ones, they are filled up with too much fat, salt and yukky stuff that you don't even want to think about.

The sausages I buy release no fat (which means there is not too much in them in the first place), they are low salt and about 95% pork meat guaranteed and are totally gorgeous!

For The Mash.

Peel and boil a mixture of white potatoes and sweet potatoes. Don't add any salt to the water. Boil until nice and soft, but not mushy. Add lots of black pepper, a teaspoon of wholegrain mustard and a handful of chopped chives. Then mash together, adding just a little milk to soften if required.
Because the sweet potato holds its moisture really well, there is no need to add butter to this dish.

Easy Onion Gravy.

Slice 1 onion, finely. Gently sauté in a little olive oil for about 10 minutes on a very low heat to add a little colour. Add gravy and stir. Simmer gently until ready to use. Easy!

Serve with piles of vegetables, I like classic broccoli and carrots. (steamed of course)

And Enjoy!

ONION GRAVY SURPRISE!

I was taking part in a television show, being filmed in front of a live studio audience, making bangers and mash with roast vegetables - the healthy way. I'm not saying I was under pressure or anything, but it was the first time I had cooked on TV, I had the director yelling down one ear telling me to look at camera 2 as I was talking but show my food to camera 1! In my other ear-piece was the producer counting me down to the advert break as I was trying to put this dish together, making it look as smooth as Gordon on a good day. I'd almost made it. Sausages, perfect. Mash looked delicious, creamy and steaming hot. I was just working on the onion gravy when the presenter asked me what the tomatoes on the side were for! Oooops aaaarh, it suddenly dawned on me that they were supposed to go in the oven with the roast vegetables. Having to quickly think on my feet I said, "Tomatoes . . . oh those tomatoes, well they erm go erm in the erm . . . gravy!"

What was I thinking? Cherry tomatoes in onion gravy, had I completely lost the plot? (The presenter obviously thought so!) Anyway, as I'd already said it, I had to carry it through. So when the time came for me to serve up the roast vegetables, sausages and mash potato, everyone waited with baited breath for me to pour the gravy. Well, as you can imagine, it didn't exactly pour, more 'plopped'. We all sat down to taste the food and do you know what . . . it was absolutely gorgeous. The tomatoes added a lovely flavour to the gravy and complimented the sausages and mash beautifully. So this has now become a regular in our house. The kids call it lumpy gravy - but for all the right reasons!!

EGG AND CHIPS!!!

Yes you heard it right – egg and chips. Isn't it the thing we all crave when coming back from our hols?. Good ole fashioned, British egg and chips. Not a dish that you would usually associate with healthy food but actually when made in this way, using fresh organic ingredients, it's a wonderful dish that provides plenty of nutrients for a healthy heart, body and definitely soul!

Serves 4

For the chips:

4 large organic white potatoes

Drizzle of Olive Oil.

'Low Salt' (Salt Substitute)

- After scrubbing well but keeping the skins on, cut the potatoes long ways into chip strips. Put in roasting tin (on to magic carpet cooking sheet - see page15) drizzle lightly with extra virgin olive oil. Sprinkle with 'Low Salt'

- Oven bake, stirring occasionally at 200°C/gas 6 for 50 mins - 1 hour until golden brown.

For the Egg and Tomato Bake

900g/2lb organic ripe vine tomatoes

3 garlic cloves, finely sliced

3 tbsp Extra virgin olive oil

2 tsp sugar

4 large free range eggs

2 tbsp chopped parsley

2 tbsp chopped chives

Sprinkle of Worcester sauce.

Black Pepper

- Pre-heat oven to 200°C / Gas 6.

- Cut the tomatoes in half and spread over base of large shallow oven-proof dish.

- Drizzle the olive oil over, sprinkle the garlic slices, add plenty of black pepper and the sugar. Give the tomatoes a good stir so that they are glistening all over with the oil and seasonings.

- Bake for 40 minutes until softened and turning brown.

- After 40 minutes, take out of oven and make 4 gaps in the soft tomatoes and break an egg into each gap. Cover the dish with foil and return to the oven for 5 – 10 minutes depending on how you like your eggs.

- Scatter with the chopped herbs and serve piping hot.

(If not serving with the chips – serve up with chunks of ciabatta bread and a fresh green salad.)

ENERGETIC

*Dishes that tantalise the taste buds
with a bit of a kick!.*

Tuna and Chicken Kebab

Smoked Haddock Kedgeree

Aromatic Filo Tomato Pastry

Mediterranean Burgers
with Spicy Tomato Salsa

Glazed Sweet Potatoes with Ginger

Chicken Curry with Sweet Onions

Speedy, Healthy Bangers and Beans

Smoked Haddock and Potato Hash

TUNA OR CHICKEN KEBAB

Served with roast baby carrots and baby courgettes

Serves 4

2 large fresh tuna steaks or 2 large, organic chicken breast portions	Juice of 1 lemon
2 tsp whole black peppercorns	4 wooden skewers (soaked in water)
2 cloves of garlic	200g baby carrots. Washed, topped and tailed
sprig of fresh rosemary	200g baby courgettes. Washed.
Extra virgin olive oil.	Celery salt
I glass white wine.	Garlic powder

For the Veg:

- Pop the washed veg in a roasting tray. Drizzle with a little olive oil.

- Sprinkle with a dusting of celery salt and garlic powder and put in the oven at 200°C for about 40 minutes.

While the veg is cooking:

- Cut the tuna steaks or chicken breast portions into chunks - about 1.5 cm.

- In a pestle and mortar, crush the black peppercorns together with the garlic, rosemary and lemon juice. Put this in a bowl together with the tuna/chicken and mix up well so that all fish/meat is covered.

- Thread the cubes of fish/meat onto the skewers.
  (soaking these in water first prevents them from splintering and should stop them from burning during cooking!)

- Next, heat up a little olive oil in a frying pan on a medium heat, carefully place the kebabs into the pan and cook for 7-8 minutes, turning so that all sides get nice and brown.

If using chicken it is so important that you check to make sure the meat is cooked right the way through. If you are using tuna steak, it's ok to have it a little raw in the centre, that's perfectly safe. I tend to switch off when the tuna is still a little bit 'pink' inside, as it continues to cook for a few minutes longer.

● Put kebabs to one side while you de-glaze the pan with the glass of white wine. To do this, simply pour in the wine, turn up to a high heat and scrape the frying pan to get all the scrummy bits.

● Serve on top of the roast carrots and courgettes, pouring over the wine glaze to finish off. Perfect with a helping of basmati rice (microwave Express Rice is fine!)

SMOKED HADDOCK KEDGEREE

Serves 4

300g un-dyed smoked haddock fillet

1 bay leaf

450ml vegetable stock, hot

1 tbsp olive oil

2 shallots, finely chopped

1/2 tsp ground cumin

1/2 tsp ground coriander

1 tsp mild curry powder

300g basmati rice, rinsed

Small strip of lemon zest and 1 tbsp lemon juice

150g shelled fresh or frozen peas

4 tomatoes, chopped

2 tbsp snipped fresh chives

- Put the smoked haddock in a deep frying pan. Add the bay leaf, then pour over the stock. Heat to simmering point, then reduce the heat, half-cover the pan with a lid and poach for 6-8 minutes until the flesh flakes easily when tested with the tip of a knife. Lift the fish out of the cooking liquid and set aside.

- Make up the volume of the cooking liquid/stock to 600ml with water and put to one side with the bay leaf.

- Rinse out the pan, then add the oil and heat over a moderate heat for a few seconds.

- Add the shallots and cook for 4-5 minutes until softened, then stir in the spices, followed by the rice. Stir for a few seconds to coat with the oil and spices, then add the reserved cooking liquid and bay leaf and the strip of lemon zest. Bring to the boil.

- Reduce the heat to a gentle simmer, cover and cook for 10 minutes. Add the peas, cover again and cook for a further 5 minutes or until the rice is tender and nearly all the stock is absorbed.

- Meanwhile, flake the fish, removing any skin and bones. Reduce the heat under the pan to very low, then gently stir the fish into the rice together with the tomatoes, lemon juice and chives.

- Season with black pepper to taste, then transfer the kedgeree to a warm serving dish and garnish with egg quarters.

FRAGRANT TOMATO FILO TART

Serves 4

4 sheets filo pastry	1 tsp cumin seeds
2 tbsp olive oil	2 garlic cloves, sliced
1/2 tsp ground coriander	1/2 tsp chilli powder
1/2 tsp fennel seeds	6 large ripe tomatoes, each cut into 4
1 onion, thinly sliced	thick slices

- Pre-heat the oven and a non-stick baking tray to 220°C/425°F/gas mark 7. Put the sliced onions in a frying pan with a drizzle of olive oil, cover with a lid and cook on a very low heat for 15-20 minutes or until starting to caramelise.

- Meanwhile, place the filo pastry sheets on top of each other on a non-stick baking tray. When the onions are starting to caramelise, add the ground coriander, fennel seeds, cumin seeds and garlic, and stir-fry until the spices start releasing their wonderful fragrance.

- Add the chilli powder and the tomatoes (you will need to do this in two batches), and cook for 1-2 minutes, being careful not to break up the tomato slices. Set aside any cooking juices.

- Arrange the tomatoes on the pastry, leaving a 5mm (1/4 in) edge to the pastry. Set the baking tray on top of the hot tray in the oven and cook for 15-20 minutes, until the pastry is crisp and golden.

- Drizzle any tomato spice juices over the tart and serve.

This dish makes a lovely light lunch or a great starter.

Tomatoes: Are a extremely good for you. As well as being delicious, recent studies suggest that lycopene, the pigment that gives tomatoes their red colour, may help prevent some forms of cancer by lessening the damage caused by 'free radicals'. Tomatoes are also a good source of potassium, (good for leg cramps) beta-carotene and vitamins C and E.

Glazed Sweet Potatoes with Ginger

Absolutely, mouthwateringly delicious.
Makes a lovely accompaniment to a
light salad or any chicken dish.

Serves 4

900g/2lb sweet potatoes

50g/2oz unsalted butter

3 tbsp olive oil

2 garlic cloves, crushed

2 pieces stem ginger, finely chopped
from jar

2 tsp ground allspice

1 tbsp syrup from ginger jar

cayenne pepper, to taste

10ml/2 tsp chopped fresh thyme, plus a
few sprigs to garnish

- Peel the sweet potatoes and cut into 1cm cubes. Melt the butter with the oil in a large frying pan. Add the sweet potato cubes and fry, stirring frequently, for about 10 minutes until they are just soft.

- Stir in the garlic, ginger and ground allspice. Cook, stirring occasionally, for 5 minutes more. Stir in the ginger syrup, a generous pinch of cayenne pepper and the chopped thyme. Stir for 1-2 minutes more, then serve in warmed bowls scattered with fresh thyme sprigs.

Mediterranean Beefburgers with Red-Hot Tomato Salsa

If you're lucky with the weather, these burgers taste best cooked outside on the bbq. However, as our weather is not always the greatest, you can still make these wonderful tasty burgers by cooking in a frying pan (no need to add any oil) under a grill or, the best option if not outside is to use a George Foreman type gadget. All of the fat runs out and you still get that 'chargrilled' effect.

Serves 4

500g lean minced beef
25g wholemeal breadcrumbs
2 garlic cloves, crushed
40g sun-dried tomatoes in oil, drained
    and finely chopped
2 tbsp chopped fresh coriander
4 wholemeal burger buns
50g rocket

Tomato Salsa
225g ripe vine tomatoes, finely diced
1 red pepper, deseeded and
    finely diced
1/2 fresh mild green chilli, deseeded and
    finely chopped
1 fresh red chilli, deseeded and finely
    chopped
2 tsp balsamic vinegar
1 tbsp snipped fresh chives
1 tbsp chopped fresh coriander

- Place the minced beef, breadcrumbs, garlic, sun-dried tomatoes and coriander in a large bowl and use your hands to mix the ingredients together thoroughly.

- Divide the mixture equally into 4 and shape into burgers about 10cm across and a similar size to the buns.

- On your hot hob, bbq or George Foreman, cook until nice and crispy on the outside and fully cooked on the inside.

- To make the salsa, mix together all the ingredients in a bowl. Season to taste. You can chop all the salsa ingredients together in the food processor to save time – just use the pulse button to get the right consistency.

- Split the buns in half and pop under the grill or onto the barbecue rack to toast lightly. Place a few rocket leaves on each base, top with a burger and add a spoonful of salsa, then replace the tops. Serve immediately.

KERRY KATONA AND THE ELDERFLOWER FIZZ CHALLENGE

I've been fortunate to work with a few different celebs, helping them understand how easy it is to eat for health. Kerry and I worked together when she was first pregnant with baby number 4. She was craving all things spicy and fizzy! I think Kerry made the mistake that many people make. They assume that eating Take-Aways won't do them any harm and that drinking fizzy sweet drinks will give them the much needed energy boost that they are searching for.

Well, the fizzy drinks will give you a boost for about 5 minutes and then your sugar levels will drop dramatically and make you feel more tired than you were in the beginning. I suggested to Kerry that she made a start by cutting out all sweet fizzy drinks (even so-called diet drinks . . . loaded with chemicals!!) and tried my Elderflower Fizz.

If you'd like to give this a go, you'll need:

1 large glass	Sparkling mineral water
1 small slurp of Elderflower cordial	A squeeze from a fresh lime.
(found in supermarkets and health food shops)	Ice.

I have to ensure that I drink gallons of water everyday, to counteract some of the side effects from my medication, and this is a drink that gives you that instant fizz and refreshing, sharp bite that we all sometimes crave. By dumping the sugar and chemical filled fizzy drinks and taking up the delightful Elderflower Fizz challenge, I promise you'll start to feel better in a an instant!

CHICKEN CURRY WITH SWEET ONIONS

1 tbsp olive oil

Knob of butter

3 onions, thinly sliced

2 green peppers, very finely sliced

2 cloves garlic, finely chopped

2 tbsp plain flour

Ground black pepper

1 tsp dried mixed herbs

1 tsp mild curry powder

6 skinless chicken breast fillets each cut into chunks

300ml/1/2 pint unsweetened organic apple juice

2 tbsp tomato purée

Serve with basmati or wild rice.

Serves 2-4

- In a large frying pan, heat the oil and butter and add the onions and green peppers and stir well.

- Cook gently for about 15 minutes until the onions are starting to soften and caramelise.

- Add the garlic and cook for another 5 minutes, stirring well again. Take the onion and garlic mixture out of the pan and put to one side.

- In a separate bowl, mix the flour, black pepper, mixed herbs and curry powder. Cover the chicken pieces in the flour mixture and shake off any excess.

- Cook in the frying pan, (with a dash of extra olive oil if needed) for about 10 minutes. Turing half way through to brown both sides.

- Pour in the apple juice and add the tomato purée. Stir really well to incorporate all of the flavours. Next return the onions and peppers to the pan, cover with a lid and cook for about 25 minutes.

- Check that the chicken is cooked right through. The sauce will thicken.

Sprinkle with a little parsley or coriander to serve.

Kerry Katona

Kerry has a love of curries, usually take-aways. The problem with so many of these meals is that apart from the very high salt and fat content, they usually have a large amount of monosodium glutamate (MSG). This may not mean much to you, but take it from me, the side effects I personally suffer whenever I unknowingly eat anything containing MSG, are so dramatic, that it's frightening. I suffer instant tachycardia (rapid heart beats) and continual palpitations for the next 5-6 hours. MSG can also cause depression, mood swings, migraine headaches etc etc.

Heart Felt Thanks To Kerry Katona

Beans, beans good for your heart,
The more you eat, the more you . . .

There isn't a week that goes by when another article published in the medical literature reports finding protection against heart disease and stroke, among other diseases, in men and women whose diets include a wide variety of fruits and vegetables. Whole-grain foods have been linked with protection against cardiovascular disease. All kinds of beans are rich in soluble fibre that effectively lowers cholesterol levels in the blood.

SPEEDY, HEALTHY BANGERS AND BEANS

'Ve added this dish in the 'Energetic' chapter just because you can spice it up as much as you like (or not!) but this is also a great dish to feed a houseful. You can very easily increase the amounts to feed many hungry mouths, yet its so quick and easy and healthy too!!

Serves 4 or increase the quantities easily to serve more!

1 tbsp olive oil	2 x 410g cans of mixed beans
8 healthy, organic sausages	(kidney, haricot etc),
(*see note on page 22)	drained and rinsed
1 onion	400ml/14fl oz chicken or vegetable stock
4 celery sticks, sliced	2 tbsp dijon mustard
3 carrots, sliced chunkily	Slurp of Worcester sauce
Handful of french beans or peas or mange tout	Handful chopped parsley

Cut each of the sausages into 4.
In a large frying pan that has a lid, heat the oil over quite a high heat. Add the chopped bangers and sizzle away for about 7 minutes or until they are browned on all sides.

Then add the onion, carrots, celery and green veg (peas or beans). Cook for another 5 minutes until onions are beginning to soften.

Next, add the drained, rinsed beans, vegetable or chicken stock and Worcester sauce. Bring to the boil and cover and cook for about 15 mins until the carrots are tender.

Finally, stir in the dijon mustard, chopped parsley and season to taste with black pepper if required.

Serve steaming hot with lots of chunky wholegrain bread to mop up the yummy sauce!

This dish is so quick and easy to make but so yummy, we all love it. I don't want you to be put off by the lack of colour in the picture. We could have made it look much more colourful by using the dyed 'yellow' smoked haddock, but I prefer to use the un-dyed fish. Give this a dish a go - and you'll be eating it out of the pan! Me? . . . Oh no, I never do that! ?

SMOKED HADDOCK AND POTATO HASH

Serves 4

Knob of butter

Drizzle of olive oil

2 onions, finely sliced

1 clove garlic crushed

1kg/2lb 4oz Maris Piper or King Edward potatoes cut into small slices

500g/1lb 2oz skinless smoked haddock, cut into large pieces

4/5 rashers of very lean back bacon, cut into thin strips

1/2 cup of frozen peas

Freshly ground black pepper

3/4 pint vegetable stock

Handful of chopped curly parsley.

Squeeze of fresh lemon to serve

Heat the oil and butter in a large, wide pan and add the onions and saute for about 7 minutes until nice and soft.

Add the crushed garlic, potatoes, bacon strip and cook for another 5 minutes, stirring well to ensure they are all coated in the olive oil and butter.

Pour in the vegetable stock and grind in a little black pepper to taste. Stir it up and add the fish pieces and frozen peas.

Bring to the boil and cover and cook for a further 20-25 minutes until the potatoes and fish are tender.

Sprinkle with chopped parsley and serve piping hot.

RELAXED

Easy, Simple, quick and gentle.
Salads – Sauces – Accompaniments

Spicy Couscous

Baby Leaks in Red Wine

Roasted Garlic Tomatoes

Baked Sweet Potato

Prawn, Avocado and Hazelnut Salad

Italian Courgettes

Black Pepper and Garlic Crush

This is a picture of me and my Mum

My mum is completely and utterly fabulous although I have to admit she didn't teach me how to cook. (I'm sure I remember her feeding a houseful of people on Marks and Spencer's individual chicken kievs. Must have cost her a fortune!)

Although she didn't teach me to cook, she certainly taught me to laugh! When I was about 5 months pregnant with my first baby I was still working as a 'jobbing' actress and got a part in a supermarket commercial filming in Amsterdam so dragged mum along with me just incase 'junior' decided to make an early appearance. Besides me having to stop my mum taking pity on all the 'lovely sweet girls' during our tour of the red light district, she embarrassed me beyond belief in the film studio. During rehearsals and practicing my lines, mum was jumping around in the background flirting outrageously with the (very handsome) Dutch director. The flirtation grew and grew until eventually mum got what she wanted all along...an invitation to be in the film! She asked the director what she should do as a background artist and he told her just to do what she normally does in a supermarket. So what did my mum do? - she shoved a can of beans up her jumper and legged it!!

SPICY COUSCOUS

2 tbsp olive oil

1 clove of garlic, crushed

1 tbsp ground cumin

1 tsp ground coriander

1 tsp paprika

350ml (12 fl oz) chicken or vegetable
  stock

Good pinch saffron strands

6 salad onions, trimmed and thinly sliced

225g (8oz) couscous

Coarsely grated zest and juice of
  1 lemon

2 red chillies, seeded and very finely
  chopped

2 tbs raisins

2 tbs pomegranate seeds, optional

50g (2oz) pine nuts, toasted

Heat 1 tablespoon of olive oil in a large pan. Add the garlic, cumin, coriander and paprika and fry over a gentle heat for 1 minute, stirring.

Add the stock and saffron and bring to the boil. Add the salad onions, and then pour in the couscous in a steady stream and give it a quick stir.

Cover the pan with a tight-fitting lid, remove from the heat and set aside for 5 minutes, to allow the grains to swell and absorb the stock.

If you are serving this warm, stir in the rest of the oil and the remaining ingredients now. Otherwise, leave the couscous to cool and chill in the fridge for 1 hour before adding all the other ingredients for a deliciously cold couscous salad.

BRAISED BABY LEEKS IN RED WINE WITH AROMATICS

12 baby leeks or 6 thick leeks

1 tbsp coriander seeds, lightly crushed

5cm piece of cinnamon stick

2 tbsp extra virgin olive oil

3 fresh bay leaves

2 strips pared orange rind

5-6 fresh or dried oregano sprigs

1 tsp sugar

1 glass fruity red wine

2 tsp balsamic or sherry vinegar

2 tbsp coarsely chopped fresh oregano
   or marjoram

Ground black pepper

If using baby leeks, simply trim the ends, but leave them whole. Cut thick leeks into 5 - 7.5cm/2 – 3 ins lengths.

Place the coriander seeds and cinnamon in a pan wide enough to take all the leeks in a single layer. Dry fry over a medium heat for 2-3 minutes, until the spices give off a fragrant aroma, then stir in the olive oil, bay leaves, orange rind, fresh or dried oregano, sugar, wine and balsamic or sherry vinegar. Bring to the boil and simmer for 5 minutes.

Add the leeks to the pan. Bring back to the boil, reduce the heat and cover the pan. Cook the leeks gently for 5 minutes. Uncover and simmer gently for another 5-8 minutes, until the leeks are just tender when tested with the tip of a sharp knife.

Use a slotted spoon to transfer the leeks to a serving dish. Boil the pan juices rapidly until reduced to about 75-90ml/ 5-6 tbsp.

Add salt and pepper to taste and pour the liquid over the leeks.

You can either serve immediately, they go wonderfully with the spicy couscous or you may prefer to leave to cool. If you chill them, bring them back to room temperature again before serving. Sprinkle the chopped herbs over the leeks just before serving.

ROASTED GARLIC TOMATOES

6 large beef tomatoes or 12 smaller
    tomatoes (organic of course)

2 cloves of garlic

2 whole bulbs of garlic

Good sprinkling of ground black pepper

Sprinkle of celery salt

2 tsp sugar

1 tbsp olive oil

1 teaspoon of mixed dried herbs

Fresh basil

- Heat the oven to 200°C/400°F

- Slice the very top off the whole garlic bulbs to expose the tops of the cloves and place in the centre of the roasting tray.

- Wash tomatoes and cut into halves

- Peel and crush the garlic cloves (or chop them very finely)

- Put the oil, garlic and any herbs into a bowl.

- Add tomato halves and stir until well coated with the oil and flavours

- Put tomatoes and oil mix in a roasting tin and sprinkle with black pepper, celery salt and sugar and place in the oven for 40-50 minutes until the tomatoes are golden on top and nicely caramelised.

Baked Sweet Potatoes

I LOVE baked sweet potatoes especially if I'm really starving. I feel I can eat a great big plateful and know that I am filling myself up with energy and goodness.

Buy only organic sweet potatoes, scrub, give a couple of stabs with a sharp knife and cook, on a baking sheet in a hot oven for about 50 minutes or until soft to the squeeze.
(I suggest that you cook on a baking sheet as sweet potatoes can 'leak' a bit during cooking)

Because sweet potatoes are much more moist than white potatoes, you will not need to add any butter, but you can be as inventive as you like with fillings.

PRAWN, AVOCADO & PECAN HERB SALAD

Serves 2

8 uncooked king prawns	Mixed salad leaves
1 clove garlic, crushed	Watercress
2 spring/salad onions, finely chopped	2 tomatoes sliced
1 tbsp soy sauce	1 handful of pecan nuts
Drizzle of olive oil	Juice from 1 lemon
Freshly ground black pepper	Handful of freshly torn basil
1 ripe organic avocado	

- Heat the olive oil in a pan, add the chopped salad onions, crushed garlic, soy sauce, black pepper and raw prawns. Saute until prawns have turned pink all the way through.

- Arrange the salad leaves, watercress, avocado and tomato in a big dish, pour over the prawns and other warm ingredients. Sprinkle with torn basil and pecan nuts and serve.

Ainsley Harriott

I could learn a lot from Ainsley. Not only is he a wonderful chef and a great television personality, he is completely and utterly in love with such a wide variety of flavours. He is passionate about them! I asked him to tell me his favourite ingredients and his list just goes on and on. I could tell his thought process was completely controlled by what his mouth was anticipating next!

I also asked what his most emotional memory relating to food was. This is what he said:

'Fairy cakes - making them with my late mum. It was the first thing I learnt to cook and of course licking the spoon afterwards. My mum was superb - she always encouraged us...'

Ainsley loves superfoods, ginger, asparagus, and prawns. So Ainsley, this salad is especially for you!

Heart Felt Thanks To Ainsley Harriott

COURGETTES ITALIAN STYLE

Serves 4

15ml/1 tbsp olive oil

1 large onion, chopped

1 garlic clove, crushed

4-5 medium courgettes, sliced

150ml/ 1/2 pint/ 2/3 cup hot home-made
chicken or vegetable stock

2.5ml/ 1/2 tsp chopped fresh oregano

Freshly ground black pepper

Chopped fresh parsley to garnish

Heat the oil in a large frying pan and fry the onion and garlic over a moderate heat for 5-6 minutes until the onion has softened and is beginning to brown.

Add the courgette slices and fry for about 4 minutes until they just begin to be flecked with brown on both sides. Stir frequently.

Stir in the stock, fresh oregano and pepper, and simmer gently for about 8-10 minutes until the liquid has almost evaporated. Spoon the courgettes into a serving dish, sprinkle with chopped fresh parsley and serve.

BLACK PEPPER AND GARLIC CRUSH

This is a great little trick for adding an intense flavour to your food. Remember you are not meant to be adding extra salt to your food, so you need to replace that flavour another way.

Make sure you have a good sized pestle and mortar. Add garlic cloves and whole black peppercorns and crush together. You may then add lemon or lime juice. Herbs add another dimension, rosemary is my favourite. Just crush it all together and use this as a dry marinade to meat or fish.

EXCITED

*Big bang! Food to feed a house full . . .
and lots of colour*

Italian Blushing Pasta

Moroccan Chicken

Paprika Pork

Mega Meatballs in Spicy Tomato Sauce

Ratatouille Chicken Tray Bake

Beef Stew with Guinness

Marinated Seabass on a bed of Noodles

Caribbean Fish Stew

Best mates - *Lela and Mima*

Italian Blushing Pasta

Serves 4 - but feel free to double up

4 large cups of uncooked pasta	Drizzle of olive oil
Approx 20 organic cherry tomatoes, halved	2/3 sprigs of fresh rosemary
	1 tsp dried oregano
2 red sweet peppers, cut into chunks	1 tsp garlic powder
8 shallots, peeled and halved	1 tsp celery salt
1 whole garlic bulb. NOT peeled	Black pepper

Before cooking the pasta, pre-heat oven to 190°C.

- On a large baking tray, place all the vegetables. Do not peel the garlic bulb but slice off the very top so that the cloves are just exposed.

- Drizzle everything with a little olive oil and dust over with the oregano, garlic powder, celery salt and black pepper. Making sure that everything is glistening with the oil and flavours but not drowning! Pop the fresh rosemary on top and put in the oven for about 50 minutes, checking and turning the peppers halfway through.

- Get your timing right so that your pasta has finished cooking at the same time as your 'blushed' vegetables. Drain the pasta and put in a big bowl. Add the vegetables and stir up, being careful not to break up the tomatoes. Squeeze the garlic out of its skin and add to dish.

Serve immediately with a green salad.

Optional Extra - I like the simplicity of this pasta dish and you can really taste the sweetness of the tomatoes. However, if you like more sauce on your pasta, you can add a couple of teaspoons of pesto.

Simon Cowell

*Lovely Simon told me he loves Italian food especially pasta, so I produced this dish especially for him. Simon is living mostly in L.A these days and eats out most of the time, but still likes to get his hands dirty in the kitchen every now and then. My Italian Blushing Pasta dish is so simple that anyone can do it. Add a big green salad and some fresh bread from the bakers and you've got yourself a party!
.....Oh if only I could sing!!*

Heart Felt Thanks To Simon Cowell

MAGNIFICENT MOROCCAN CHICKEN

Inspired by my good friend Mida x

This recipe is perfect to cook in a 'Tagine', but don't be put off if you don't have a Tagine, you just need a large strong saucepan or casserole dish that is suitable for the hob-top, that also has a lid.

Traditionally, this dish is made using preserved lemons, although you could use fresh, the preserved ones give that authentic Moroccan flavour. They can usually be found in any of the big supermarkets although they are sometimes well hidden – so get someone to hunt them out for you!

Serves 4-6

1 chicken, 3-4 lbs, cut into 8 pieces
(Or 6 chicken breast portions if you prefer)
2 tsp paprika
1 tsp ground cumin
1 tsp ground ginger
1 tsp turmeric
1 tsp cinnamon
Freshly ground black pepper
2 tbsp olive oil
3 cloves garlic, minced
1 onion, finely sliced

2 preserved lemons, rinsed in cold
 water, and halved
1 cup green olives, pitted
1 pint chicken or vegetable stock
1/2 cup raisins
1/2 cup canned chick peas
1 glass white wine.
1 handful chopped fresh coriander
1 handful chopped fresh flat-leaf parsley

- Combine all the spices in a large bowl. Pat dry the chicken pieces and put in the bowl, coat well with the spice mixture. Let the chicken stand for one hour in the spices.

- In a large frying pan or non-stick saucepan with lid, heat the olive oil on medium-high heat. Add the chicken pieces and cook for about 7 minutes until browned on all sides. Lower the heat to medium-low, add the garlic and onions. Cover and let cook for 15 minutes.

- Add the white wine, lemon halves, olives, raisins, and stock. Bring to a simmer on medium heat, then lower the heat to low, cover, and cook for an additional 35-45 minutes, stirring regularly, until the chicken is cooked through and tender.

- Mix in fresh chopped parsley and coriander just before serving.

Serve with couscous or rice

Paprika Pork with Fennel and Caraway

Serves 4

15ml/1 tbsp olive oil

4 boneless pork steaks

1 large onion, thinly sliced

1 clove garlic, crushed

400g/14oz can chopped tomatoes

5ml/1 tsp fennel seeds, lightly crushed

2.5m/ $^1/_2$ tsp caraway seeds, crushed

Good sprinkling of fresh rosemary

15ml/1 tbsp paprika,
   plus extra to garnish

30ml/2 tbsp soured cream

Freshly ground black pepper

Noodles tossed with poppy seeds,
   to serve

- Heat the oil in a large frying pan. Add the pork steaks and brown on both sides. Lift out the steaks and put them on a plate.

- Add the onion to the oil remaining in the pan. Cook for 10 minutes until soft and golden. Stir in the tomatoes, fennel seeds, caraway seeds, rosemary, paprika and garlic.

- Return the pork to the pan and simmer gently for 20-30 minutes until tender. Season with plenty of pepper. Lightly swirl in the soured cream and sprinkle with a little extra paprika.

Serve with brown rice cooked as packet instructions and sliced steamed courgettes or other green steamed vegetables.

This is a lovely easy dish and makes a nice change from chicken! Very tasty, low fat, NO salt and when served with brown rice and steamed green vegetables provides a filling nutritious meal that will keep you topped up for hours!

Remember - if I can make these dishes - you can make these dishes. There may be some ingredients that you don't recognise, but give them a go - you just might love it!!

Mega Meatballs in Spicy Tomato and Vegetable Sauce

Serves 4

For the Meatballs:

500g/1lb Lean steak mince

2 onions, finely chopped

3 cloves garlic, finely chopped

1 tsp dijon mustard

1 tsp ground allspice

1 tsp cinnamon

1 egg

freshly ground black pepper

For the sauce:

2 tbsp olive oil

1 large onion chopped

3 courgettes, diced

2 large red peppers, chopped

2 x 400g/14oz tin plum tomatoes

150ml/5 fl oz tinned tomato passata

1 tbsp Worcester sauce

1 tbsp balsamic vinegar

2 cloves garlic, finely chopped

1 teaspoon dried oregano

1 handful basil leaves, torn

To make the meatballs, put the steak mince, chopped onions, garlic and mustard, spices and egg into large bowl and mix together well. (Using hands is usually the easiest way.) Divide mixture into 8/10 and shape into balls. Sauté in a dash of olive oil over a medium heat, for about 15 minutes. Transfer them to a plate and keep warm.

Preheat the oven to 180°C/350°F/gas mark 4.

To make the sauce, heat the olive oil in a saucepan and sauté the onion and garlic until softened. Add the courgettes and peppers and sauté for a further 10 minutes, stirring occasionally. Add the tomatoes, passata, and all remaining ingredients, and simmer for about 10 minutes.

Pour the sauce into a large casserole dish. Arrange the meatballs in the sauce, cover and cook in the oven for 20 minutes, or until the sauce is bubbling and the meatballs are piping hot. Garnish with the basil leaves and serve immediately.

My Personal Favourite!

Perfect for freezing. Serve with rice, pasta or jacket spud. uuummm.

RATATOUILLE CHICKEN TRAY BAKE

Serves 4

600g/1lb 5oz baby new potatoes, halved

2-3 tbsp olive oil

4 chicken breast portions

4 leeks, rinsed and cut into 4

1 green pepper, chopped

1 red pepper, chopped

1 yellow pepper, chopped

200g/7oz organic cherry tomatoes

2 organic parsnips, quartered long ways

2 organic carrots, cut into chunks

2 cloves of garlic, crushed

handful fresh rosemary

Sprinkle fresh thyme

1/2 tsp garlic powder

1/2 tsp celery salt

Juice and zest of 1 organic lemon

Ground black pepper.

- Preheat the oven to 180°C/200°F/Gas mark 6.

- Mix the lemon zest with the herbs and crushed garlic. Lightly slash the chicken portions using a sharp knife and rub mixture all over and into the chicken.

- Put the new potatoes, chicken and all vegetables on a large roasting tin. Drizzle with olive oil and lemon juice. Season lightly with black pepper, garlic powder and celery salt.

- Roast for 25 minutes, stir everything around, then add the cherry tomatoes and stir again so that everything browns evenly, and then roast for another 25 minutes.

- Check that the chicken is cooked through by piercing the thickest part of the joints with a sharp knife: The juices should run clear.

Make life easy - bung it all in !

BEEF STEW WITH GUINNESS

This is a stew without dumplings - making it healthy and guilt free!

1 kg best quality super lean stewing steak	1 bouquet garni
6 rashers lean back bacon	350 ml (12 fl oz) Guinness
10 – 12 shallots, halved	1/2 pint beef or vegetable stock
1 red pepper	1/2 tbsp sugar
1 green pepper	Slurp of Worcester sauce
3 tbsp olive oil	Ground black pepper
1 tbsp plain flour	

- Pre-heat oven to 150°C/300°F

- Cut meat into 3-4 cm cubes, trimming off any excess fat. Put flour and black pepper in bowl and add cubed meat. Make sure meat is well dusted with the seasoned flour.

- In a frying pan, heat the olive oil over a medium heat and add the meat. Brown on all sides. You may need to do this in 2 batches. Once browned, put the steak into the casserole dish.

- Cut the bacon into cubes and put this and the chopped onion into the frying pan and brown off for about 5 minutes. Add this to the casserole. Now add the chopped peppers, ground black pepper and bouquet garni to the casserole.

- Return the frying pan to the heat and add the Guinness, tomato purée, Worcester sauce and sugar, bring to the boil and pour over other ingredients in casserole. Add enough beef or vegetable stock to cover the meat and a little bit more!

- Cook in the oven for about 3 hours, stirring every now and then, until the meat is lovely and tender.

- Serve piping hot with yummy mashed potato.

Max Clifford

When I first met Max Clifford, I really didn't know what to expect. I understood that he had a persona that is seen on TV, but of course I know that looks can be deceptive. Max has a reputation for being tough, for taking risks and for speaking his mind.

When I first met him, I found all of the above to be true. I also found that he is incredibly kind, committed to every good cause he feels he can help. He is fair, loyal and has a fabulous sense of humour!

Max told me that his favourite dish from his childhood was beef stew and dumplings.

'Money was very tight but we were hungry kids. My mum used to make a delicious stew with dumplings. It was cheap to make but would go a long way. The taste still takes me back now . . .'

So Max, this one's for you, with love.

Heart Felt Thanks To Max Clifford.

Dani's Marinated Seabass on a Bed of Noodles . . .

2 small fresh seabass, about 900g-1kg
   total weight, filleted

For the marinade:

1 small onion, diced

1 clove garlic, crushed

1/2 tsp ground coriander

1/2 tsp ground cumin

1/2 tsp hot chilli powder (optional)

2.5cm fresh root ginger, peeled and
   finely grated

1 tbsp clear honey

Juice of 1 lemon

2 tbsp olive oil

Freshly ground black pepper

● Rinse and dry the fillets. Place the marinade ingredients into a shallow dish and mix together, then add the fillets and cover with the marinade. Leave in the fridge for up to 2 hours if possible.

● Preheat the oven to 220°C, gas mark 7. Line a roasting tin with enough foil to make a generous envelope. Grease the foil with a little olive oil, add the sea bass fillets and any remaining marinade. Fold over the edges of the foil to create a puffed-up, sealed envelope and bake the fish for 20 minutes or until the flesh is firm. Remove from the oven and leave to rest for a further 3 minutes.

● Remove the fish from the foil and place on warmed serving plates on top of a bed of freshly cooked noodles (made as per packet instructions). Pour over any remaining cooking juices and serve.

The Gorgeous Girls story

It was a hot, hot summer when I was in hospital recovering from my attacks and the 'Gorgeous Girls' came to visit. (The gorgeous girls being my very best girlie friends . . . not so called because we think we're beautiful but because "gorgeous" became one of our much used and loved phrases!). There are four of us in the gorgeous girl gang. Elly, Dani, Charlotte and me. We pride ourselves on the fact that between us we have 11 children! And none of us would be seen dead at the school gates without a spot of lippy on!

On about day seven of my recovery, the gorgeous girls came to visit me in hospital. Elly was wearing a white linen suit, long auburn hair down to her waist, Dani sported tight jeans, sexy little top, blond hair. Charlotte had on a halter neck sundress, white, with big red cherries on it . . . and matching lipstick! The reason I explain all of this is because it's important that you can picture the scene. A sombre yet busy cardiac care ward full of seriously ill heart patients. Death was constantly evident and so the tone of the ward was very hushed, with only whispers spoken. I was lying quietly in bed, still hooked up to my heart monitors, feeling pretty sorry for myself. In the distance I could hear the clip clopping of Charlotte's kitten heels down the corridor. I could also hear quiet nervous giggling. I heard the girls ask the nurse where I was and then hurry along to my bedside. Elly was the first to put her head around my curtain, big grin on her face and in a rather too loud voice, so that the whole ward could hear, said…."bloody hell, nearly gave myself a heart attack finding this place!"

Gorgeous Girls - I love ya! x

Caribbean Fish Stew

Grated zest and juice of 1 lime

2 x 6 – 8oz skinless white fish fillets such as cod, haddock or hoki

6 cooked king prawns

Juice of 2 lemons

1/2 pint of vegetable stock

3 tbsp tomato purée

Handful fresh thyme leaves stripped away from the stalks

1 tbsp dark rum

3 tbsp olive oil

1 onion cut into rings

handful of parsley, chopped

2 garlic cloves, crushed

1 beefsteak tomato sliced (or equivalent smaller ones)

2 tsp dark muscovado sugar

Fresh lime halves to serve

- Spread the lime zest and juice over the base of a shallow dish. Lay the fish in the bowl and pour over the lemon juice.

- Using a mortar and pestle, crush the thyme leaves, 2 tsp olive oil and 1/2 tsp of black peppercorns making a paste. Rub the paste all over the fish and then sprinkle over the rum. Cover and marinade for about an hour.

- Heat the olive oil in a deep frying pan and fry the onion for 4-5 minutes until soft. Add the chopped parsley, garlic and sugar and cook for about 4 minutes.

- Now add the tomato, prawns and the fish with the marinade to the pan, pour over the stock and tomato purée and cook gently for 8 - 10 minutes until the fish is cooked through and flaky.

- Season with a little more black pepper and serve with the lime halves and chunky wholemeal bread.

Alison Steadman

Alison Steadman is one of my very favourite actresses. She has some lovely 'foodie' memories, particularly toasting buns in front of an open fire and then 'putting best butter and jam on' whilst enjoying a pot of tea.

One of her favourite dishes is Fish Stew. Good Choice. Alison says any fish will do and I agree. Feel free to alter the fish you use in this dish.

"A little bit of what you like is good for you"
Prawns are quite high in cholesterol so limit to once or twice a month. However this dish is otherwise very good for you, so don't worry . . . just enjoy!

Heart Felt Thanks To Alison Steadman

THE SECRET INGREDIENT

I know we'd all like to take a magic pill or take a sip of tincture that will make us healthier and help us lose weight. Wouldn't it be wonderful if that pill could also reverse our heart disease, stop us from getting cancer, make us look younger, sleep better and actually make our whole lives happier, easier and hopefully longer.

Well there is something that will do all of the above, but it is not taken in the form of a tablet. You don't even need to get it on prescription. And it is actually not so secret after all, although many people seem to have problems realising how easy it is and how fast the benefits will come.

The Secret ingredient is simply increased physical activity. There's nothing like it and there's nothing that will replace it!

I'm not necessarily talking about joining a gym or getting into some pink and purple lycra, leg warmers and 'feeling the burn' but I do practice what I preach and I call it 'Active Living'.

When I first came out of hospital, all I could manage were a few steps to my front gate. My little boy wanted me to pick him up from school like all the other mums but I actually couldn't manage the 5 minute walk. So I had to be inventive to keep up appearances. I would spend all day getting ready. I'd have a shower – sleep for 1 hour. Dry my hair – exhausting work, so sleep for 2 hours. Add a bit of lippy – another quick nap and it'd be time to go. Because I couldn't manage the walk, I'd get a lift around the corner to the school. I would then settle myself on the school bench before all the parents arrived and when they did, I would smile and wave as if everything was completely normal. I did catch a few looks, as if to say, "I thought she was meant to be ill, she looks OK to me!" I would then manage to stand up to greet my little man as he ran out of school, and give him the big hug that he'd been waiting for. Luckily, he was then happy to be walked home by a friend, he didn't seem too bothered that I didn't actually walk him home, only that I was there to see him when he first came out of the door. I would then sit back down on my 'life-saving' bench and wait for all the other parents to go before I'd catch my lift back home again.

Baby Step by Baby Step.

Each time I did this little journey I was left completely exhausted and adding to this challenge, I also had a 9 month baby girl and a very active 2 year old at home. For obvious reasons I had to have a full time nanny for a while to do all the physical stuff, but I even found talking to the little ones incredibly tiring. However, because I had started to push myself, baby step by baby step, I soon realised that I was getting stronger. I knew my heart was very damaged, and none of the doctors could give me a positive prognosis for survival at this stage, but thankfully, I started to tune into my body and listen to what it was telling me. When I felt strong enough I started to walk for maybe 3 or 4 minutes. Other days I could only manage 1 or 2. Little by little, step by step, I built my strength to the level that I'm at now.

Would you be surprised to hear that I now exercise EVERYDAY. I swim, I walk, I cycle with the kids. I don't do anything very dramatic, I keep my heart rate nice and steady, I allow myself to get gently out of breath but never gasping and I still listen to my body. When it tells me its time to stop and rest, I do just that. If I feel I can do a bit more, I'm no longer afraid to give it a go.

The good news is that it works. My cardiologists are amazed at my recovery. They cannot believe the levels of fitness that I have achieved and the way my heart is responding. I know I'll never run a marathon, and I know I have a time limit on my exercise so that I don't over-do it. (20 minutes seems to be my magic number), but I also am happy that I have taken control of my 'active living' and it is having such a positive effect on my health that I wouldn't want to live my life any other way.

So back to the 'secret' ingredient, why don't you try a bit of active living yourself. Enjoy your food, eat for health by following some of my recipes then go for a walk. Make a resolution to begin today. Start by just taking a walk around the block. Then build it up slowly, listening to your body. Walk as though you are late for an appointment. When you're on the telephone, walk around instead of sitting still. Go for a wander in the park at lunch time. Do your grocery shopping in half the time it usually takes you. And before you know it, you will start to lose a little weight, you'll start to feel a bit more energetic, and you'll probably want to try some other activities. Things like biking, hiking, swimming, gardening, dancing, and anything else you enjoy that will get your heart rate up.

Promise yourself you'll live actively for three months. If you can honestly say after that trial period that you don't feel 100% better, then quit. But you will feel better, and you won't quit.

Lyndas Story.

I met Lynda while giving a counselling session at one of my heart groups. She was morbidly obese and already had suffered 2 heart attacks. She was told that the third one would kill her unless she lost weight. She was scared, tearful and desperate when she told me that she had tried every diet on the planet and they just didn't work. No surprise there then! So I gave her a list of my recipes, and taught her how to eat for health first. And I suggested she went for a little walk everyday. That was it. How simple!

I met her again after 3 weeks and she had lost almost a stone and she was smiling! It was wonderful to see. Because she was being properly satisfied by her meals she had managed to cut out all the junk she was eating before but still felt full up. And because the food she was now eating was giving her sustainable energy, she said that she actually felt like taking a walk after her meal instead of taking a nap! I continued to give her recipes to keep her interested, and 18 months later, Lynda is no longer obese, she looks about 20 years younger and she's found herself a toyboy! You go girl !!

The Secret Ingredient.
Try it, you'll like it!
I promise

IMPATIENT

No need to dial a pizza – healthy, happy meals ready in a flash.

Fish in a Bag – 'ready meal'

Chicken Risotto parcel – 'ready meal'

Snappy Tuna Melt

Steak Dijon

Wild Mushroom Herby Omelette

Carrot and Butternut Squash Soup

Mozzarella on Toast

Smoked Haddock Chowder

FISH IN A BAG

Makes 1 'ready meal'

1 x 200g/7oz white fish fillets, skinned
(cod or haddock or hake – whatever
   takes your fancy!)

Juice of 1/2 lemon

Tbsp olive oil

Handful of flat-leaf parsley, roughly
   chopped

1 garlic clove, sliced or crushed

2 sage leaves

1 sprig of rosemary

1 bay leaves

2fl oz white wine vinegar

Freshly ground black pepper

- Preheat the oven to 150°C/300°F/Gas Mark 2.

- Place each fish fillet on a large square of foil and drizzle over the lemon juice and olive oil.

- Place all other ingredients over the fish and wrap the fillets in the foil to make a securely sealed parcel. Bake for 20/25 minutes.

This is a perfect dish to prepare in advance and keep in the fridge. The healthiest 'ready meal' in the world. No more processed food need pass your lips when you are in a hurry!

Chicken Risotto Parcel

A 'ready meal' with none of the hidden salt or sugar. You can chuck all the raw ingredients in the foil parcel in the morning, pop it in the fridge and then just bung in the oven when you get home from work. You can then unwind for an hour, have a soak, chat on the phone and 'ping' the timer goes off and you have the most delicious, nutritious ready meal on the planet!!

Serves 1 (but of course you can make as many as you like!)

1 chicken breast portion	1 tbsp tomato purée
4-5 mushrooms, sliced	Dash or Worcester sauce
4-5 cherry tomatoes	Sprinkle of dry mixed herbs
drizzle of olive oil	Sprinkle of garlic powder
1½ ounces (38g) long-grain rice	Black pepper
6 tbsp of chicken stock	

Pre-heat oven to 400°F/ 200°C

Prepare a large piece of foil by folding in half to give extra strength.

Mix all ingredients together in a bowl.

Put all ingredients into centre of foil. Fold up the sides to produce a bowl effect and fold over the top to seal the edges securely.

Place on a baking tray and cook for 45 minutes.

SNAPPY TUNA MELT

Serves 2

Nutty wholemeal chunky bread	**To Serve**
1 tbsp olive oil	**Watercress or mixed salad leaves**
1 clove garlic, crushed	**Sliced avocado**
1 red pepper deseeded and finely diced	**$1/2$ cucumber, diced**
2 spring onions, thinly sliced	
2 tomatoes very finely chopped	
300g can tuna in spring water, drained	
Black pepper	

Optional -
   Thinly sliced cheese or avocado.

- Toast the chunky wholemeal bread on both sides – put to one side.

- Heat the olive oil in a pan, and over a moderate heat sauté the garlic, spring onions, and pepper. Cook for 5-6 minutes until soft.

- Add the chopped tomatoes, tuna and black pepper, cook for another 3-4 minutes until heated through.

- Pile tuna mixture onto pre-prepared toast.

Optional, you can add a little cheese or sliced avocado if you really fancy!
Pop under a hot grill for just a couple of minutes to melt together.
Lovely!

This dish is as easy as they come but so perfectly tasty!
Tinned tuna is rich in vitamins D and B12.

WILD MUSHROOM OMELETTE WITH FRESH HERBS

Serves 1

25g/1 oz butter

About 125g/4 oz wild mushrooms, chopped

Freshly ground black pepper

Fresh herbs, such as tarragon or parsley, chopped (optional)

3 eggs

- Heat half of the butter in a small saucepan and sauté the mushrooms for a couple of minutes. Add a little seasoning and the herbs. Remove the pan from the heat.

- Meanwhile, break the eggs into a bowl and beat them lightly with a fork. Place the remaining butter in an 18-20cm/7-8 in omelette pan over a high heat. As soon as the butter begins to foam, add the beaten eggs and cooked mushrooms and leave for about 10 seconds.

- Using the back of a spoon, stir the omelette mixture lightly and then flip in half. Cook for another 10-15 seconds, tip onto a warmed plate and serve.

Remember you can add pretty much anything into this omelette: ham, cheese, any vegetables.

FAST FOOD

I am always amazed by peoples lack of imagination when it comes to 'fast food' Instead of hitting the burger bar or fish and chip shop, or eating a chocolate bar c bag of crisps, try some wholemeal pitta, popped in the toaster and low fat humous Or this omelette recipe takes less that 5 minutes to prepare and cook! My kids love omelettes, and I'm happy for them to snack away on one whenever they fancy Fast food, simple food at its best.

STEAK DIJON

Red meat isn't an ingredient that is classed as particularly healthy. My attitude though is that life is short and if there is something that you really love, you absolutely MUST treat yourself every now and again! Lean steak meat has iron which is beneficial to all of us, and served up with a big salad or plenty of vegetables, this dish is a winner.

Bruce Forsyth
"*nice to see you, to see you nice*"

Bruce Forsyth

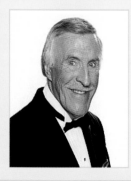

Bruce donated his recipe for steak Dijon as served at the Wig and Pen Club, London.
When I asked his favourite meal, Brucie said,
"Lasagne – The first meal my wife (Wilnelia) cooked for me. It was delicious – I thought, she's not only the most beautiful woman I've ever met – BUT SHE'S ALSO A WONDERFUL COOK!!! What a lucky man!"

Heart Felt Thanks To Bruce Forsyth

FORSYTH'S STEAK DIJON

As formerly served at the Wig and Pen Club, London

Ingredients:
Sirloin steak
English mustard
Demerara sugar

Method:
- Grill both sides of a sirloin steak
- On one side spread a generous amount of English mustard
- Sprinkle Demerara sugar on top of the mustard, again be very generous
- Put under a very hot grill until the sugar starts to bubble and caramelise
- Serve with new potatoes and a salad or vegetables of your choice

Hope you enjoy it!

Bruce Forsyth

CARROT AND BUTTERNUT SQUASH SOUP

This soup is so quick and easy to make, wonderfully good for you and will keep for up to a week in the fridge.

Serves 4

1 red onion, finely chopped
2 garlic cloves, finely chopped
2 tbsp olive oil
4 large carrots, peeled
1 medium butternut squash, peeled and deseeded

Freshly ground black pepper
2-3 thyme sprigs, leaves picked
Handful chopped fresh parsley or coriander
1½ pints chicken or vegetable stock

- Sweat the onion and garlic in the olive oil over a medium heat for about 7 minutes until soft.

- Chop the carrots and butternut squash up into about 1.5 cm cubes and add to the pan. Season with black pepper and cook for another 10 minutes until the vegetables start to soften.

- Pour in the stock, add the thyme leaves and parsley or coriander and bring to the boil. Now turn down the heat a little and simmer for about 30 minutes.

- Finally, use a hand blender or liquidiser to smooth the soup.

Emma Thompson

Emma's favourite ingredients are used in most of my recipes and happen to have a good health benefit, thats probably why she always looks so wonderful!

When I asked her what her emotion memory relating to food was, she said,

'My Father loved to melt cheese on a tin plate and mop it it up with bread and Worcester sauce. However - he died at 52 of heart disease, so I try to avoid it!!'

Heart felt thanks to Emma Thompson

Cheese on toast is a favourite for lots of people but it can clog up those arteries. If you love cheese on toast, one way to make it healthier is to use low fat mozzarella. Just grill this on top of toasted wholegrain bread. You can add tomatoes, Worcester sauce or a little mustard for a bit of a kick. Tastes just as good and has around half the fat content!

91

SMOKED HADDOCK CHOWDER

Serves 2

1 onion, chopped	418g can creamed corn
1 clove garlic, crushed	4 tbsp milk, or to taste
2 potatoes, scrubbed and sliced	1 handful parsley, chopped
500ml / 18 fl oz vegetable stock	Freshly ground black pepper
2 smoked haddock fillets, about 100g/4oz each, skinned and cut into chunks	

- Put the onion, garlic and potatoes into a large sauté pan. Pour over the vegetable stock and simmer for about 8 mins until the potatoes are soft, but still have a slight bite.

- Add the chunks of smoked haddock, the creamed corn and half of the milk - if you prefer thinner chowder, add more. Season with a little black pepper.

- Gently simmer for 5-7 mins until the haddock is cooked (it should flake easily when pressed with a fork).

- Sprinkle over the parsley and serve with chunky wholegrain bread.

MORE HEALTHY

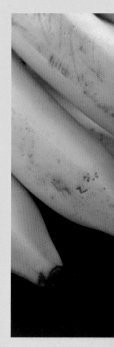

FAST FOOD!

INVENTIVE

Surprise yourself!
Try something new today

Healthy Spring Vegetable Risotto

Chilli Con Healthy!

Baked Crusty Fennel

Peppered Lemony Monkfish

Sicilian Tomatoes

**Seared Scallops with Butternut
and Parsley Mash**

Cajun Chicken Salad

HEALTHY SPRING VEGETABLE RISOTTO

Serves 4

1 litre vegetable stock

100g asparagus tips

100g baby carrots, halved lengthways

200g fresh young peas shelled

500g baby broad beans, shelled

2 tbsp olive oil

2 baby leeks, thinly sliced

300g risotto rice

1 tbsp fresh pesto
 (supermarket bought is fine)

25g pine nuts, toasted

- Bring the stock to the boil in a large saucepan, then reduce the heat, add the asparagus tips, carrots, peas and broad beans and simmer for 4-5 minutes until tender.

- Remove the vegetables with a draining spoon and set aside. Keep the stock simmering over a gentle heat.

- Meanwhile, heat the oil in a large, heavy-based frying pan and add the leeks. Stir-fry for 2 minutes until they are bright green, then stir in the rice.

- Add 2-3 tbsp of the hot stock and cook gently, stirring until the liquid is absorbed. Continue adding the stock, a little at a time, until the mixture is soupy and the grains of rice are tender but still have a slight bite. This will take about 20 minutes.

- Stir in the pesto and season to taste. Gently stir in the asparagus, carrots, peas and beans and cook for a few more minutes until the vegetables are heated through.

Serve in warmed dishes. Sprinkle over the pine nuts to serve.

Dr Chris Steele

I met Dr Chris when I appeared on 'This Morning' to talk about my experiences. He showed a great understanding of my situation and had some helpful hints about coping with an uncertain future. He has since been diagnosed with heart disease himself and so I hope he is surrounded with people that will offer him the same kind of support he offered to me.

Dr Chris told me that he loves Chilli Con Carne which can be really healthy if made in the right way and served up with a great big fresh salad . . . well, the next time I see you Dr Chris, I'm going to make you a big bowl full !X

Heart felt thanks to Dr Chris Steele

CHILLI CON HEALTHY

Extra virgin olive oil	Pinch of cayenne pepper
1 large onion, finely chopped	1 x 14oz can chopped tomatoes
2 garlic cloves, crushed	1 level tbsp tomato purée
2 fresh chillies, deseeded and chopped	1 pint beef stock
2 tsp ground cumin	Freshly ground black pepper
1 tsp ground coriander	1lb extra lean beef, minced
1 tsp paprika	1 x 14oz can red kidney beans, drained

Dry fry the minced beef until brown. Drain off any fat. Add a splash of olive oil and then add the onion and garlic and cook gently until softened.

Add the chillies and all the spices and continue frying, stirring occasionally, for 2-3 minutes.

Add the canned tomatoes, tomato purée and stock. Stir well and bring to the boil. Reduce the heat and simmer gently for 15 minutes, until the liquid is slightly reduced.

Season with pepper and add the drained kidney beans. Heat through gently for another 30 minutes, adding a little extra stock if required.

Serve hot, sprinkled with chopped coriander leaves, and basmati rice or a fresh green salad.

p: A dollop of low fat natural yogurt on the top is extremely tasty and, if you've one overboard on the chilli, it's a great way to "cool" things down!

BAKED CRUSTY FENNEL

Serves 4

3 fennel bulbs, cut lengthwise into
   quarters

30ml/2 tbsp olive oil

1 garlic clove, chopped

50g/2oz day-old wholemeal
   breadcrumbs

2 tbsp chopped fresh flat leaf parsley

Ground black pepper

- Cook the fennel in a pan of boiling water for 10 minutes.
  Preheat the oven to 190°C/375°F

- Drain the fennel and place in a large earthenware baking dish or baking tray
  then brush with half of the olive oil.

- In a small bowl, mix together the chopped garlic, wholemeal breadcrumbs
  and chopped fresh flat leaf parsley, then stir in the rest of the olive oil. Sprinkle
  the mixture evenly over the fennel, then season well with black pepper.

- Bake the fennel for about 30 minutes, or until it is tender and the breadcrumb
  topping is crisp and golden brown. Serve the baked fennel hot, as an
  accompaniment to any meat or fish dish.

PEPPERED LEMONY MONKFISH

Serves 4

2 tbsp vegetable oil

1 onion, finely chopped

2 red peppers, deseeded & thinly sliced

2 yellow peppers, deseeded & thinly
 sliced

175g sugarsnap peas

500g monkfish fillet, skinned and cut into
 4cm chunks

Grated zest and juice of 1 lemon

1 tbsp black pepper and garlic crush
 (see page 57)

Handful fresh basil, finely shredded

- Place the monkfish chunks in a bowl with the black pepper and garlic crush. Marinade for 10 minutes or so.

- Heat a wok or large frying pan over a high heat and add 1 tbsp of the oil. Add the onion and stir-fry for 1 minute. Stir in the peppers and sugarsnap peas and continue stir-frying for about 5 minutes. Remove the vegetables to a plate using a draining spoon.

- Add the remaining oil to the pan and add the marinaded monkfish and stir-fry on a gentle heat for about 4 minutes, carefully turning the chunks so as not to break them up, until the fish is cooked through and flakes easily.

- Add the lemon zest, lemon juice and return the stir-fried vegetables to the pan to heat through, stirring for 2-3 minutes. Scatter over the basil and serve at once.

Try serving with a sachet of 'express rice'. Great if you're in a hurry!

SICILIAN TOMATOES

Firm round beef tomatoes are perfect for this dish. Making a tasty snack or a meal accompaniment, the taste of the Mediterranean is as wonderful as ever. Feel free to swap the chicken for tuna fish!

Serves 4-8

8 beef tomatoes	1 tbsp fresh oregano or marjoram
2 tbsp olive oil	2 tsp capers, chopped
1 medium onion, very finely chopped	4 black olives, chopped
1 clove garlic, crushed	Freshly ground black pepper
15g pine nuts	Dash of Tabasco
50g wholemeal breadcrumbs	25g low fat mozzarella cheese
175g cooked chicken, finely chopped	

Pre-heat the oven to 180°C

Slice the top off each tomato and scoop out the pulp and seeds, chop and reserve these for later.

Heat the oil in a pan and add the onion, garlic and pine nuts for about 7 minutes.

Stir in the breadcrumbs and chicken. Cook for a further couple of minutes. Remove from the heat and stir in the oregano or marjoram, capers, olives and black pepper. Now add the tomato pulp and the dash of Tabasco. Give it all a good stir.

Spoon the mixture back into the tomato skins and add a thin slice of mozzarella on top of each tomato.

Place on a baking tray and cook for 30 minutes until tender and cheese has turned golden. Serve hot or cold.

SEARED SCALLOPS WITH BUTTERNUT AND PARSLEY MASH

Serves 2

250g/9oz scallops

Juice and zest (finely grated) from 1 lime

1 tsp fresh ginger root, finely grated

2 tbsp soy sauce

350g / 12 oz butternut squash, peeled, deseeded and cut into chunks

350g / 12oz potatoes peeled and cut into chunks

50g / 1 oz low fat soft cheese

freshly ground black pepper

1 sprig fresh thyme, (lemon) or chervil, to garnish

- Put the scallops into a shallow, non-metallic bowl with the lime zest, lime juice, ginger and soy sauce. Stir well, cover and marinate for 20 minutes.

- Meanwhile, cook the butternut squash and potatoes in boiling water for about 20 minutes, until tender. Drain well, mash thoroughly, then beat in the low fat soft cheese. Season with black pepper. Keep warm over a very low heat, stirring occasionally.

- Heat a char-grill pan or non-stick frying pan. Add the drained scallops and cook for about 2 minutes on each side. Avoid overcooking them as they can quickly toughen.

- Share the mash between 2 warmed plates and serve with the scallops, garnished with sprigs of chervil or lemon thyme.

Ingrid Tarrant

Ingrid loves reindeer meat with boiled potatoes and cranberry sauce! Ingrid is from Norway and it always reminds her of home. Unfortunately she doesn't get to go back as often as she would like but whenever she does get a chance, reindeer meat is always the meat she most looks forward to having.

No matter how hard I tried I just couldn't come up with a reindeer meat recipe! Sorry!

So, instead for Ingrid I've chosen another popular Nordic dish, scallops. This is a perfect, easy dish for anyone who hasn't tried scallops before but fancies giving them a go. Enjoy!

Heart felt thanks to Ingrid Tarrant

QUICK CAJUN CHICKEN SALAD

Serves 4

4 chicken breast portions	**Fresh green salad leaves**
2 tbsp cajun spice mix	**Lemon to serve.**
Drizzle of olive oil	

Cut each chicken breast portion in half, long ways and dust with the cajun chicken spices. Leave to marinade for 10 minutes in the fridge to get the full flavour.

In a frying pan, drizzle a little olive oil and cook the chicken for 7 - 8 minutes, turning half way through, ensuring that the chicken is cooked thoroughly all the way through.

Serve on a bed of green leaves with a little lemon squeezed over the top.

You can make this into a more filling meal by serving with rice or pasta.

Linford Christie

Linford Christie OBE is a former athlete, and the only British man to win Olympic, World, Commonwealth and European 100m gold medals. He still holds the UK record.
When I asked him about his favourite food, health and 'superfoods' were top of his

list. I guess being an athlete makes you much more aware of how food can affect your body, although taste was really important to him as well. He remembers tastes from his childhood with banana porridge that his grandmother used to make being the strongest memory. He also loves chicken with 'all the flavours' so Linford, I hope this Cajun Chicken dish tickles your taste buds . . .

Heart felt thanks to Linford Christie

Puddings . . .

I'm often asked if I have any recipes for 'healthy' puddings and I usually struggle with this. Apart from the obvious - fresh fruit salad and possibly yoghurt, puddings are generally loaded with butter and/or sugar so its difficult to come up with something that could be classed as healthy and tasty.

However, I do have a philosophy on this subject that I feel sure you're going to like.

"Life is short and puddings are delicious! Therefore, once you have cut out all the junk, and all the processed food and you are confident that you are giving yourself and your family the best health benefits through the great food that you eat, you deserve a treat. And if there is a scrumptious, delicious, gorgeous pudding that is winking at you, begging to be tasted then go for it!
Just not everyday and not with every meal!

Sir Ranulph Fiennes

Sir Ranulph Fiennes, is a record breaking adventurer and holder of several endurance records. He was the first man to visit both the north and south poles by land and the first man to completely cross the Antarctic by foot!

Sir Ranulph has suffered a heart attack and endured bypass surgery and amazed everyone by competing in seven marathons in seven days very quickly after-wards. Probably not to be recommended - however, still an amazing achievement.

When I asked him what his emotional connection to food was, he told me this story:

"My late wife Ginny of 36 years marriage, taught me to make choc sauce out of Mars bars, Nescafe grains and milk. Delicious! She died in 2004 and I think of her and so many happy meals whenever chocolate sauce is around"

Well isn't that what life is all about? Memories. Eating well, living well and being happy.

Heart Felt Thanks to Sir Ranulph Fiennes

Being Ill Is Getting Better

Even though it takes a good long time to recover from any health scare or emotional trauma, and the journey can be a bumpy one, anyone who has come through to find light at the end of the tunnel will tell you that life does eventually return to normal. A different kind of normal, possibly even a better 'normal' than before.

Although I wish my heart attacks hadn't happened, especially when I was so young and my babies, well, such babies, I honestly cannot say that my life is worst because of what happened, in fact I would probably go as far as saying that my life is richer because of what happened to me. Maybe its because I have realised what amazing family and friends I have. I have learnt to identify those who give and those who take. In turn I have identified which type of person I want to be and I think much more about my place in this world, and the impact that I have on my family, my friends and my planet. I may not be here for quantity, none of us know that for sure, but I'm certainly going for quality. Everyday is a precious gift, and although I worry for the future, I am happy in the knowledge that I'm doing the absolute best I can do. And I know it's not much, but I hope my book helps you to enjoy some happy, healthy mealtimes with your precious loved ones! x